Dear Family and Friends of Young Readers,

Learning to read is one of the most important milestones your child will ever attain. Early reading is hard work, but you can make it easier with Hello Readers.

Just like learning to play a sport or an instrument, learning to read requires many opportunities to work on skills. However, you have to get in the game or experience real music to keep interested and motivated. Hello Readers are carefully structured to provide the right level of text for practice and great stories for experiencing the fun of reading.

Try these activities:

• Reading starts with the alphabet and at the earliest level, you may encourage your child to focus on the sounds of letters in words and sounding out words. With more experienced readers, focus on how words are spelled. Be word watchers!

• Go beyond the book — talk about the story, how it compares with other stories, and what your child likes about it.

• Comprehension — did your child get it? Have your child retell the story or answer questions you may ask about it.

Another thing children learn to do at this age is learn to ride a bike. You put training wheels on to help them in the beginning and guide the bike from behind. Hello Readers help you support your child and then you get to watch them take off as skilled readers.

— Francie Alexander
Chief Academic Officer
Scholastic Education

For Jules Arthur and Oliver Jamie,
and all the lovely flowers
in all the colors of the rainbow
that help to make the earth so beautiful.
–J.H.C.

ISBN 0-439-44162-5

12 11 10 9 8 7 6 5 4 3 2 1   3 4 5 6 7 8/0

Printed in the U.S.A.
First printing, April 2003

Bright Yellow Flower

by Judith Hoffman Corwin

Hello Reader! Science — Level 1

SCHOLASTIC INC.

New York   Toronto   London   Auckland   Sydney

Mexico City   New Delhi   Hong Kong   Buenos Aires

It's spring!
It's time for me to bloom.
I am a bright yellow flower called
a daffodil.

The sun warms me up.
The sun keeps me strong.

Sunlight is very important to me.

I need sunlight, air, and water
to grow.

I don't grow from a seed.
I grow from a bulb.
It stores food.
Its roots get water from the soil.

My flower has six petals.
They smell sweet in the breeze.

My flower's center is called the
trumpet.

My stem helps me stand straight.
It holds my flower toward the sun.
It also carries food from my bulb
to my flower.

My flower has six petals.
They smell sweet in the breeze.

My flower's center is called the
trumpet.

My stem helps me stand straight.
It holds my flower toward the sun.
It also carries food from my bulb
to my flower.

It is raining.
Rain is good for me.
My roots drink up the water.

Splash!
Splash!
Splash!

The rain stops.
Here's my friend the butterfly.

Flutter!

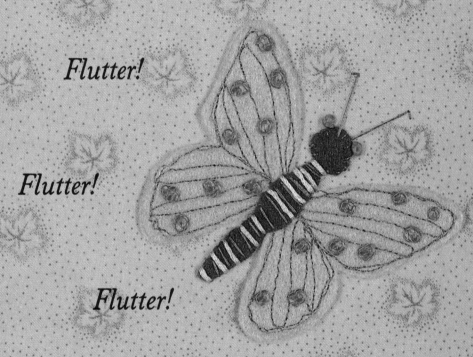

Flutter!

Flutter!

She likes my bright color and
sweet smell.

Buzz!

Buzz!

Buzz!

It's a helpful
bee.

He collects my fuzzy pollen
to make honey.

There's a spider.
She's spinning a web on my leaves
to catch some bugs.

Spin!
Spin!
Spin!

A ladybug is on my leaf.
She eats insects that might
hurt me.

Munch!

Munch!

Munch!

She makes me smile.

Little mice jump in the grass.

A leaping frog is looking for lunch in the nearby pond.

A red robin is flying by, with straw in her beak.
She is busy building her nest.

Finally, it starts to get dark.
A hedgehog is running around.
He has a mouthful of grass and
leaves.

A cat lies down to spend the night. Tomorrow is another day for me— the bright yellow flower!